CASTLES | *Old Stone Poems*

To the Zappitellos and the Tufekçis
— J. P. L.

For Elizabeth Harding, royal agent and friend
— R. K. D.

To my family, for allowing me to indulge in my childhood dreams
— D. B.

The poems "Dürnstein Castle"; "Castle of Gripsholm"; "Olavinlinna Castle"; "Chillon Castle";
"Edinburgh Castle"; "Tower of London"; "Chambord"; "Hearst Castle"
copyright © 2006 by Rebecca Kai Dotlich

The poems "Bodiam Castle"; "Alnwick Castle"; "Bunratty Castle"; "Himeji Castle";
"Bran Castle"; "Catherine's Palace"; "Schloss Neuschwanstein"; "The Castle in the Air"
copyright © 2006 by J. Patrick Lewis

The poem "Take a castle and its legends"
copyright © 2006 by
J. Patrick Lewis and Rebecca Kai Dotlich

Illustrations copyright © 2006 by Dan Burr

Library of Congress Cataloging-in-Publication Data
Dotlich, Rebecca Kai.
Castles : old stone poems / by Rebecca Kai Dotlich and J. Patrick Lewis;
illustrated by Dan Burr.— 1st ed.
p. cm.
Includes bibliographical references and index.
ISBN-13: 978-1-59078-380-1 (alk. paper)
1. Castles—Poetry. I. Lewis, J. Patrick. II. Title.
PS3554.O773C37 2006
811'.54—dc22
2005037905

WORDSONG
An Imprint of Boyds Mills Press, Inc.
A Highlights Company

815 Church Street
Honesdale, Pennsylvania 18431

CASTLES

Old Stone Poems

J. Patrick Lewis & Rebecca Kai Dotlich

ILLUSTRATIONS BY Dan Burr

Honesdale, Pennsylvania

Contents

*T*ake a castle and its legends,
take a princess and her court,
take a king who gobbles power
like the cook's gooseberry torte.

Stir in battle, greed, and envy
to the flood of blood and tears.
Add a dungeon's hapless prisoners.
Toss in silk, grand chandeliers.

Brew the beauty of the parapets,
the spires' afterglow—
what splendor did the maid see
from that window long ago?

Add crown jewels, treason, ransom
to a kettle full of fear
as you feast on days and knights
and sip a sampling of them here.

Bodiam Castle

ENGLAND

The French are coming,
The French are coming!
King Richard cried in alarm.
Sir Edward Dalyngrigge rebuilt
The castle to keep it from harm.

Mysterious Bodiam Castle,
Floating upon a pond,
Is round and square, famed in the fair
East Sussex and beyond.

Medieval, cries the courtyard,
Medieval, the towers and moat,
Where knights advanced with lances
And the villains were cutthroat.

The castle walls were twice attacked
In treacherous days of old.
Today they sleep and mutely keep
Their secrets pigeonholed.

Tower of London

ENGLAND

Down the road from London Bridge
And Pudding Lane and Puddle Dock
There dwells a place of infamy—
Of dungeon chain and chopping block.

Here jealous kings and wicked queens
Descended stairwells seething.
Off with her head!—simple as that.
Beheadings as easy as breathing.

The grim and gloomy tower
Saw King Henry VIII decide
To end the life of his young wife,
Sad maidens at her side.

Down the road from London Bridge
And Puddle Dock and Pudding Lane,
Lovely Anne Boleyn weeps tears—
Chilling as winter rain.

Alnwick Castle

ENGLAND

They lived here through the cavalcade of years—
A dowdy duchess who refused to die,
Chandlers lighting the candle chandeliers,
A one-eyed stable boy, a Danish spy,
Silk merchants from Morocco and Tangiers,
The Scottish lord who claimed the English sky.

What names are all but memories in dust?
Empress Matilda—willful child bride,
Mad dukes, eccentric earls, and lords who must
Have traded their allegiance as the tide
Of battles made a mockery of trust.
Northumberland was cruelly occupied,

Despite the tranquil scene that here survives,
By English folk a lot like you and me.
But we live in the cottage of our lives,
And they lived near a castle by the sea.

Edinburgh Castle
SCOTLAND

A castle calls from Princes Street
Like a page from a storybook.
Out of a forest, splendors rise—
Stone and stair and nook.

A cobbled road runs far below
Where dauntless soldiers scaled walls
To stake their bloody right to dine
Inside banquet halls.

Behind your iron gates are ghosts
Of those who wrote, who came to sing;
A room where Mary, Queen of Scots,
Bore her Scottish king.

If kings had hearts, they surely cried
For every gruesome battle fought;
And Scotland cheered for jewels found
By Sir Walter Scott.

Dürnstein Castle

AUSTRIA

The village bells of Dürnstein toll,
the Danube River runs below,
medieval burg of ancient stone
sits high upon this hill.

The brothers Grimm wrote fables near,
old fairy tales spiced with fear,
enchanted by a countryside
spun of mist and magic.

In Dürnstein's fortress sat a king,
with thoughts of freedom vanishing,
held England in his prisoner's heart
and dreamed of London rain.

Soon songs and silver set him free;
while Leopold was serving tea,
a loyal servant, strong and true,
came singing out his name.

The very air (and its perfumes—
a scent of rose?) still haunts those rooms
and hints of a king who mourned lost nights
stolen from Austria's stars.

Chillon Castle
SWITZERLAND

The air is mild.
The sky, a soothing
alpine blue
here at Montreux.
Hear the waterfall?
A calming song for my stone chateau;

clear as the clang of cowbells, ah!
Beguiling bliss.

My days roll on like this.
Swans swim at my feet.
Waves lap at my door.
But there is more—
footsteps drum my empty halls;
night falls

on bell and battlement.
I am still here …

Hemmed by lake,
stunned by stars.
Swiss angels whisper

Bonivard.

Bunratty Castle

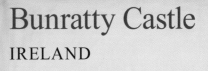

IRELAND

'Twas beside the River Ratty
That the castle was first built.
Take a history lesson, laddie:
There was blood in buckets spilt.

Tom de Clare in Norman armor
Put his stamp upon the stone,
And I'll wager that this charmer
Was a baddie to the bone.

Came the clan of MacNamaras,
Waging war upon the law—
You would think the Irish air was
Bracing for a brouhaha.

They were followed by O'Briens,
Friends and enemies who fought
Like the Christians and the lions
Did without a second thought.

But today they'll be a-tasting
Tea at Durty Nelly's Pub
As if nothing ever happened
At the good Bunratty Club.

Himeji Castle

JAPAN

Its architects erected it for war,
Its architecture is a sigh of peace,
Its tenants would continually increase
Its grandeur from the century before.

Its beauty is the white heron in flight,
Its history is a never-ending book,
Its roofs slope up like sun-picked petals.
Look!
Its gardens beg the moon to whiten night.

Its windows pierce the sky like hushed haiku,
Its walls are built of Japanese ghost stories,
Its halls recall its sorrows and its glories.
It bows as you are coming into view.

Bran Castle

ROMANIA

I am the Gothic Castle Bran.
Am I the castle of the man
The world knows as Count Dracula,
Vampire of Transylvania?

They say he haunted my house once
Performing most unusual stunts—
The Count who loved to take blood counts
In very, *very* large amounts

And made his nightly bedtime check
By neck and neck … and neck … and neck!
Could that tiptoe tall tale be true?
Open these doors, drink in the view.

Olavinlinna Castle

FINLAND

By bridge, by beam, by load of brick,
Sir Erik Tott erected it
on Swedish soil, but oh, the fight—
with Russia and our Danish knight,

because the border is, at least,
a little off. By north? By east?
(Final word of world leaders:
Russia wins by kilometers.)

Either way, the tale remains
of a tree that grows, and when it rains,
blood-red berries weep for the small
maiden buried in the wall.

But for now, a flask of wine!
A shake of salt, malt beer—divine!
Dive into a platter of breaded fish.
A feast of sugarloaf; a dish

of pudding for the guests; a feast
made with rich, imported yeast.
And now to dance. To pipe, to song!
In Finland, where brave hearts belong.

Chambord

FRANCE

As castles go, it was *the cream of* …
a French chateau to only dream of;
a hunting lodge in fancy France
alive with rumors of romance.

A masterpiece of spire and terrace,
a sprawling site the size of Paris.
The reverie of a pining king,
the girl he once loved, his rose of spring.

Leonardo, rare genius, inspired a staircase
that wound round and round to the top of the place.
Invitations to ladies to dance and to dine
came penned from a castle King Francis called *mine*.

A house full of Frenchmen would rule and die
where hundreds of chimneys crept into the sky.
As castles go, it was *the cream of* …
a French chateau to only dream of.

Castle of Gripsholm

SWEDEN

The Swedish sun rose late
then set too soon upon
this palace on the lake;
      four cannons mounted on

King Vasa's slender towers
that drank from moon and sky …
where brothers (his own sons)
      were brought to die.

A third son, Karl, came;
built windows into walls.
Lit the prison up with sun
      to warm the drafty halls.

Glancing over quiet coves,
grieving dowager queens
drew yellow drapes of Chinese silk,
      kept hearts of fallen kings

whose names spill forth in scribbles
(old characters in stone)
on stairwells scratched in hieroglyph,
      these lords by blood and bone.

Catherine's Palace
RUSSIA

I fished this pool with local boys—
What's up, lads? (Kak zhivu?)—
And looked into the palace face,
Embarrassingly blue.
I skated through enormous rooms
In paper shoes with strings
And heard *echo   echo   echo*,
Ravings of queens and kings.

I asked the doorman and the guard,
I asked a tourist why
A Russian queen would need a bed
The size of Italy.
As winter melted on the few
Who stayed to gawk at gold,
I helped a woman kneeling by
The castle in the cold.

Schloss Neuschwanstein

GERMANY

Once upon a time there was a king,
Who hid from his unhappiness in dreams
Of German knights and sagas, so it seems,
As if that glory gone were everything.

To overcome sadness and loneliness—
His madness was town gossip and well known—
He built a castle out of hope and stone,
Two mammoth pieces in a game of chess.

The only art that moved Ludwig like this
Estate were operas Richard Wagner wrote.
They met one day, posterity will note:
For Wagner it was joy; for Ludwig, bliss.

Each fell in love with what the other said,
Remarking how they found each other great
And classified all others second-rate.
Then, satisfied, they each went off to bed.

When full moons fall upon that balcony,
Mad Ludwig's ghost appears, so legends tell.
All he surveys is like some magic spell
That only now brings him serenity.

Hearst Castle

UNITED STATES

Guests, behold, if you will,
William's *Castle on the Hill*!
Built of mountain, bay, and sky,
Sir Prince of Print shall occupy.

No battles here, no soldiers slain.
No captured palace to regain.
Those Hollywood ladies and movie star gents
arrived for parties, not punishments.

They came to dance, to dine, to laugh
with grazing zebra, tall giraffe.
Picture them there—warm evenings in June,
kissed by a California moon,

in the kingdom carved with American joy—
at the Castle of William, rich newspaper boy.

The Castle in the Air

A VIKING LEGEND

Brave Eriks, Princes I and II,
Stout heroes, set out to pursue
Heaven on earth, the Odainsaker quest.
In times stark, violent, barbaric,
Denmark and Norway each sent an Erik
To find utopia by peace possessed.

Across a distant bridge there sat
A dragon chewing on dragon fat,
Licking his lips for a tasty dish of prince.
Erik II, gripped in huge claws,
Could not escape the hideous jaws
That swallowed him! But many decades hence

Norway's Erik rose once more—
Illusion was that dragon lore—
And knew he'd found the fiery gateway where
Eternal summer's sweet perfume
Of star-enameled flowers bloom.
The gods had hung a castle in the air.

A ladder swung—a cloudy chain—
To Odainsaker's glittering plain.
But time teaches what humans seldom learn:
An airy castle's splendid view
Is not the same as traveling to
True paradise, a land of no return.

Bodiam Castle *East Sussex, England, c. 1066*

Ever since the fateful year 1066, there has been some form of house for all seasons at Bodiam. In the aftermath of the Norman Conquest, when William, duke of Normandy, was proclaimed king of England, the Saxon hall was confiscated by a Norman family, the Bodenhams.

More than a castle, Bodiam has been called an "old soldiers' dream house." Its 14th-century builder, Sir Edward Dalyngrigge, had an ego to match a king's. King Richard II granted a license to strengthen the manor house against the invasion of the French. But Dalyngrigge's main goal was to build a monument "graceful, noble, and proud"—just like himself!

Have you ever seen a castle that looks like it's floating on a lake? Don't be fooled. Bodiam actually has a very wide moat. Despite this barrier, there are too many weaknesses in the castle's defenses to believe that it was ever a convincing fortress. Nevertheless, it was attacked twice: in the 1340s and during the English Civil War (1640s).

Today, Bodiam Castle is visited annually by more than 170,000 people. *—J.P.L.*

Tower of London *London, England, 1078*

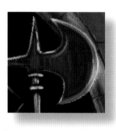

The Tower of London saw some of the most tragic executions of medieval time. One famous beheading was that of Chidiock Tichborne, a young man (some historians put his age at merely seventeen) who took time to write an elegy (a poem about death) and a letter to his wife the night before his execution.

Many of London's wealthiest kept their money and jewels in the Tower for safekeeping. During the Great Fire of London in 1666 (which started in the house of the king's baker on Pudding Lane), no doubt they sighed with rich relief; the Tower was saved while much of the city was destroyed.

This is where King Henry VIII, in a very bad mood, had his young wife, Anne Boleyn, beheaded on Tower Green, the Tower's main courtyard.

In 1483, two young princes (the brothers of York) were brought to the Tower by their uncle, Richard III, and were never seen again. It is said that their small ghosts still haunt the castle.

In 1816, a guard reported seeing a ghostly shadow limping up the stairwell of the Tower at midnight. Legend says the guard was so shaken that he died of shock. Now that's midnight madness.

If you are brave at heart, visit the Chapel Royal, where at least sixty men and women (dukes and queens among them) are entombed—all but nine seem to have lost their heads. *—R.K.D.*

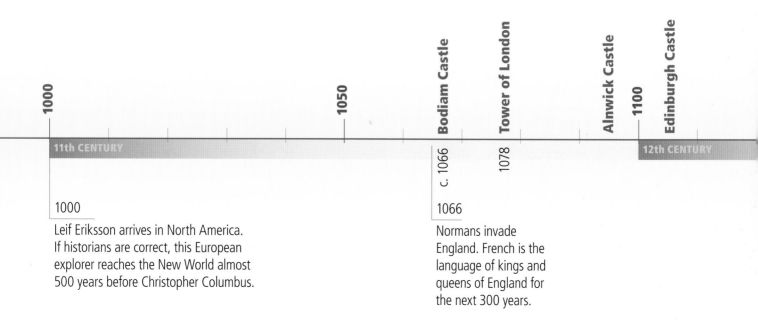

1000

1050

Bodiam Castle c. 1066

Tower of London 1078

Alnwick Castle

1100

Edinburgh Castle

11th CENTURY 12th CENTURY

1000
Leif Eriksson arrives in North America. If historians are correct, this European explorer reaches the New World almost 500 years before Christopher Columbus.

1066
Normans invade England. French is the language of kings and queens of England for the next 300 years.

Alnwick Castle *Northumberland, England, 11th century*

The early history of the castle is a tale of possessions lost and regained. In the 13th century, the castle suffered from the ongoing conflict between Scotland and England, which was unsuccessfully attacked in 1297 by the celebrated Scottish hero William "Braveheart" Wallace.

When Alnwick and its estates, in 1309, were sold to Henry Percy, the patriarch of one of England's most powerful families, English history passed into its most notorious, dramatic, and intrigue-ridden period.

For several years in the 17th century, the whole of Northumberland, including Alnwick, was occupied by the Scots, unhappy with their treatment by the king. Like so many other conflicts, this one ended in bloodshed and beheadings.

Because of its similarity to the castle of Great Britain's royal family, Alnwick has earned the nickname "the Windsor of the North." Its name is pronounced "Annick," and it is the second-largest inhabited castle in England.

Did you know that Alnwick Castle was turned into the Hogwarts School of Witchcraft and Wizardry for the Harry Potter movies? One of the most stunning scenes in the second film depicts Harry crash-landing a flying car in the castle's inner bailey, or court.   —*J.P.L.*

Edinburgh Castle *Edinburgh, Scotland, 12th century*

Did you know that a baby can be a king? In a drafty room of this castle, Mary, Queen of Scots, gave birth to a boy who was crowned king of Scotland at the age of thirteen months. (Little James later became king of England, too. Oh, baby!)

Mary was later beheaded by Elizabeth I, the daughter of Henry VIII. Like father, like daughter.

The fabled Crown Jewels (crown, scepter, and sword) of Scotland were locked away in a sealed room of Edinburgh Castle. Mystery was, exactly which room, and where? Good thing Sir Walter Scott snooped around over one hundred years later and discovered them.

Famous pied pipers, writers, and musicians of the time frequently stopped here for supper. Now that's fine dining.

Want access to your brother's room? Do what the Scots did when they ambushed Edinburgh to take it back from the English: unload a pile of corn stalks (you might substitute dirty laundry) in the doorway so it can't be closed. Enter!

It's like Halloween every day in Edinburgh Castle. The roof of the great hall is supported by huge beams carved with masks of human and animal faces. How appetizing (or spooky)!   —*R.K.D.*

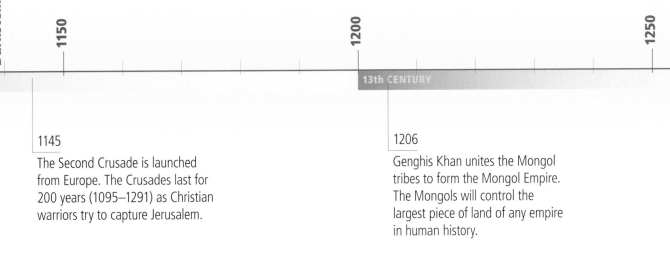

Dürnstein Castle

1150   1200   1250

13th CENTURY

1145
The Second Crusade is launched from Europe. The Crusades last for 200 years (1095–1291) as Christian warriors try to capture Jerusalem.

1206
Genghis Khan unites the Mongol tribes to form the Mongol Empire. The Mongols will control the largest piece of land of any empire in human history.

Dürnstein Castle *Dürnstein, Austria, 12th century*

The town of Dürnstein is a rare find—the tiny village actually has two castles! Dürnstein Castle (sometimes called the Kuenringer Castle after the powerful family that built it) is a hilltop fortress now in ruins. Schloss Dürnstein, on the other hand, is a newer castle that looks like a palace. Mansion or rubble: which address would you prefer?

Austrians call Dürnstein Castle a burg. (And no, that's not a nickname for a sandwich.) The term means "fortress," or fortified structure, so though it was a castle, it was built for defense, not luxury.

The burg's strength meant that holding prisoners was a snap. The most famous of Dürnstein Castle's inmates was Richard "the Lionheart," the English king who earned his nickname through tales of strength and bravery. His deeds were so well known that even Robin Hood called him his favorite king.

Legend says that after Leopold, duke of Austria, imprisoned King Richard, the king's faithful minstrel, Blondel, rode from castle to castle, singing songs familiar to the king. When Blondel came to Dürnstein, Richard recognized the music and sang along from his castle cell. The king was set free. ... Of course, England did kick in that little ransom of silver.

In 1630, over four hundred years after Richard's jail time, the beautiful Schloss Dürnstein appeared along the Danube River. People believe that this newer castle, well below the burg on a hill, inspired the brothers Grimm to write some of their bewitching tales.   —R.K.D.

Chillon Castle *Montreux, Switzerland, 13th century*

This tranquil castle sits along the waters of Lake Geneva. Some villagers say that among peaceful waterfalls, the Swiss Alps, and swans swimming in waters below the castle, the low moans of prisoners can still be heard on clear winter nights.

François Bonivard had the unlucky fate of being imprisoned here for six long years in the 16th century. He was chained to a dungeon pillar below water level in the company of rats!

Lord Byron, romantic English poet, wrote his famous poem "The Prisoner of Chillon" upon hearing the tale of Bonivard's imprisonment after he visited the castle in 1816. He then engraved his own name into the very stone pillars to which Bonivard was shackled three hundred years before.

Chillon's dungeons were actually carved right out of the rock that supports the castle's foundation. Imagine how cozy that was!

During the plague known as the Black Death, hysteria was widespread. So little was known about the disease that officials imprisoned people in Chillon after accusing them of poisoning the water.

Age defying! Chillon is said to be the best-preserved castle in all of Europe.   —R.K.D.

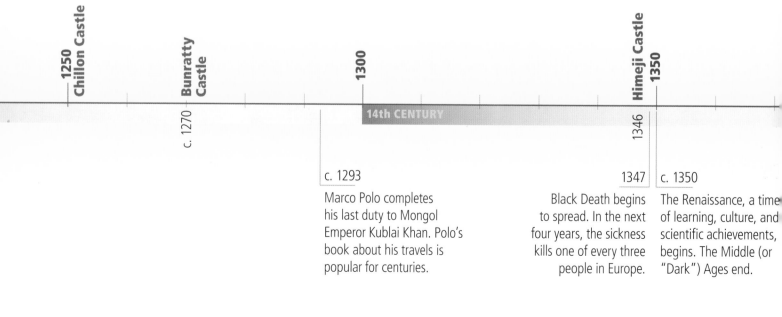

1250 Chillon Castle

Bunratty Castle c. 1270

1300

14th CENTURY

Himeji Castle 1350 | 1346

c. 1293
Marco Polo completes his last duty to Mongol Emperor Kublai Khan. Polo's book about his travels is popular for centuries.

1347
Black Death begins to spread. In the next four years, the sickness kills one of every three people in Europe.

c. 1350
The Renaissance, a time of learning, culture, and scientific achievements, begins. The Middle (or "Dark") Ages end.

Bunratty Castle *County Clare, Ireland, c. 1270*

Rebuilt at least eight times, Bunratty Castle has a history written in blood and gore. Of the many vain and vicious rogues responsible for this bloodshed, Thomas de Clare stands out. This governor of London built Bunratty in 1270 in an effort to gain power. He soon found that *holding* power was even trickier.

Ireland was parceled out among many warring clans with names like the MacGormans of Ibrickan, the O'Connors of Corcomroe, the MacNamaras of Clancuilen, the de Burghs and the O'Kellys of Connaught, and the O'Briens of Thomond. Imagine living in a land of constant local strife, much like the great feud between the Hatfields and McCoys in the American South. All that violence meant that new owners didn't have much time to settle in.

One of the only known burning executions in Ireland took place at Bunratty Castle. The victims, two men, were accused of sorcery and heresy.

A thousand years ago, there lived in these parts a lady who led a fascinating life. Through the most unusual circumstances, she came to invent an elixir called poteen (moonshine) that became famous all over Ireland. Today her house still welcomes travelers who have come to seek the so-called curing powers of Durty Nelly's drink. —*J.P.L.*

Himeji Castle *Himeji, Japan, 1346*

Some Western castles can give you the chills, literally! Cold, damp, and gloomy. You have a surprise waiting for you in Himeji-jo's delicate rooms. Guests say the castle feels like home but without the air conditioning. By the way, the Japanese suffix *jo* means "castle."

Himeji was built in 1346 and, throughout its history, was owned by thirteen warrior families. Preserved from fire and never attacked, the castle was ravaged by a destructive storm in the early 20th century. Restoration, begun in 1934, was stopped during World War II and resumed thereafter. Today, the castle is designated a National Treasure.

Princess Sen was married in Himeji Castle when she was only six years old. As legend has it, she still haunts the gardens in her wedding gown.

A servant named Okiku once overheard a plot to kill the lord and claim the castle. When Okiku told her tale, the plotter got his revenge by stealing a dish from the lord, who blamed it on Okiku and had her thrown down "Okiku's Well," not far from the castle. People say that, if you listen closely, you can still hear the screaming that drove her former master insane. —*J.P.L.*

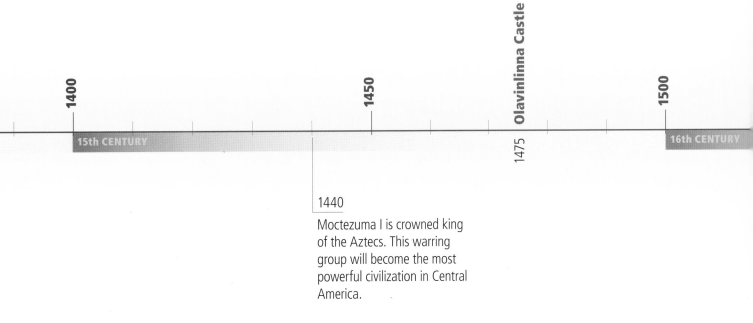

Olavinlinna Castle

1400   **1450**   1475   **1500**

15th CENTURY   16th CENTURY

1440

Moctezuma I is crowned king of the Aztecs. This warring group will become the most powerful civilization in Central America.

Bran Castle *Brasov, Romania, 1378*

For almost one thousand years, a fortress has sat on a rocky peak in Romania's Transylvania, home to the Carpathian Mountains. Today the mountaintop is occupied by Bran Castle, also known as Dracula's Castle. (As it happens, the actual Castle Dracula is in ruin on a secluded site near the Arges River.)

Legend says that beneath Bran Castle (in Slavonic, *brana* means "gate") there are miles of underground passageways. No maze map exists, and no one has ever seen these passageways, but townsfolk have kept those rumors flying for centuries.

Who was the cruelest man who ever lived? Well, Vlad "the Impaler" Tepes deserves dishonorable mention. He inspired Bram Stoker to write the novel *Dracula* and lived briefly in Bran Castle but only as a guest. In the mid-15th century, Vlad became famous for his brutal punishments, ordering people to be skinned, hacked, boiled, strangled, nailed, decapitated, blinded, hanged, roasted, and buried alive.

Everything about Bran Castle—from the dragon figures on the door handles to the brutal memory of Vlad the Impaler (Dracula to you and me)—says Keep Out!　　　　—*J.P.L.*

Olavinlinna Castle *Savonlinna, Finland, 1475*

Olavinlinna Castle was named after patron Saint Olaf and retains the fond nickname "Saint Olaf's." The castle sits on an island in the Kyronsalmi inlet in Finland. Some refer to the fortress as a phantom of the past.

Gossip from the castle kitchen: legend has it that a black ram was once raised in the castle as the main course for the St. Olaf's Day supper. Instead of ending up on the celebrated platter, it slipped from the castle wall and drowned in the stream below.

A feast fit for all! In the dining hall, guests were most likely served suppers of swan and pudding of porpoise. (Makes pizza sound *so* good.)

The Swedish crown fought with Russia for many years over this castle, which stands on land that is now Finland. Russia won; the castle indeed sprawled over what was then Russia's border ... by five kilometers. Picky, picky!

It is said that a beautiful young maiden was hidden in the castle walls for her own protection during a battle. Unfortunately, the ones who knew her hiding place were killed—and so she remains there still. Not the best way to play hide-and-seek.　　　　—*R.K.D.*

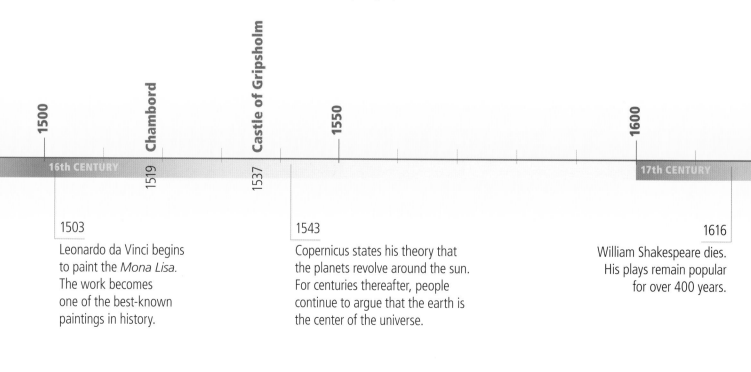

1500 | Chambord **1519** | Castle of Gripsholm **1537** | **1550** | **1600**

16th CENTURY | 17th CENTURY

1503
Leonardo da Vinci begins to paint the *Mona Lisa*. The work becomes one of the best-known paintings in history.

1543
Copernicus states his theory that the planets revolve around the sun. For centuries thereafter, people continue to argue that the earth is the center of the universe.

1616
William Shakespeare dies. His plays remain popular for over 400 years.

Chambord *Loire Valley, France, 1519*

Talk about vain. Young King Francis I had his initial *F* chiseled in stone, not once, but hundreds of times, covering the entire ceiling of the castle.

You won't need a coat at Chambord. You'll stay plenty warm by any one of the 365 fireplaces. Cozy up and listen carefully—you might hear the echo of King Francis reading poetry to one of his ladies. Romance, not war, was his sport.

Originally built to be both a hunting lodge and a castle, Chambord was a magnificent retreat for French kings and horsemen. Stables accommodated over one thousand horses, and acres of woods and rivers surrounded the site, making it a hunter's paradise.

Florentine artist and visionary engineer Leonardo da Vinci often stopped by to sketch elaborate designs for the castle, the most famous being a double-helix staircase that spiraled like twin corkscrews. That gave Chambord an interior design that was a *step* above.

Art lover that he was, King Francis saved his pennies to buy himself a special present—the *Mona Lisa*. He purchased it from the artist himself, Leonardo da Vinci, for four thousand gold coins. What a steal.

Some say when da Vinci lay dying in 1519, the king was cradling the artist's head.   *—R.K.D.*

Castle of Gripsholm *Mariefred, Sweden, 1537*

During the damp Swedish winters, the sun rises late in the morning and sets early in the afternoon. This makes for long, cold nights. Cheery.

Adding to the gray mood, Gripsholm does not have many regular-sized windows, as most are narrow defense portals built in the event of an attack.

Gustav Vasa became king of Sweden after a bloody struggle for liberation from the Danish. He promised to build a Swedish army and to back the power of the nobility.

The sons of King Vasa didn't throw punches, they threw each other in prison. In fact, Gripsholm is best known for this sibling rivalry. Is that any way to show brotherly love?

Karl IX was Vasa's third and most accommodating son. While the other two brothers were fighting, Karl put his time to better use, building windows into castle walls and installing a primitive type of central heating.

Dowager, or widowed, queens were exiled to Gripsholm. One such queen, Maria Eleonora of Brandenburg, kept her husband's heart in a silver box after he was killed in the battle of Lützen.

In the banister of the staircase are crafted symbols of the royalty who were important to the castle's history. At the bottom of the staircase is a stone etched with runes (characters of a mysterious alphabet) and at the top, the monogram of King Gustav VI Adolf.   *—R.K.D.*

1650

1700

1750

18th CENTURY

1692

Large numbers of men and women are "proved" to be witches in Salem, Massachusetts.

Catherine's Palace *St. Petersburg, Russia, 1762*

Originally little more than a stone house, the palace assumed its present-day magnificence because of the powerful Catherine the Great. Construction was completed in 1796, the year of her death.

A larger-than-life personality, the queen was so vain that she was afraid someone would discover she wore a wig. So she kept her hairdresser in an iron cage in her enormous bedroom for three years. That's one sure way to stop gossip!

Tsarskoye Selo (Tsar's Village), where the palace is located, was renamed Pushkin in 1937 to honor the famous Russian poet Alexander Pushkin (1799–1837).

Invaded in World War II, the ransacked palace was used as an army barracks by the Nazis, but not before all art collections had been evacuated inland. When the Germans finally retreated in January 1944, they destroyed what remained of the palace. The Russians later restored the building to its pre-war glory.

The three-story façade runs for twelve hundred feet and is said to be the world's longest. It's probably also the only building in the world that is robin's-egg blue. When the building was first painted such a striking color is unknown.

Visitors to any museum in Russia are required to slip paper shoes over their footwear to protect the floors.

—*J.P.L.*

Schloss Neuschwanstein *Bavaria, Germany, 1869*

After a troubled youth, Ludwig II became king of Bavaria when he was only eighteen. Wildly popular because of his age and good looks, he was one of the most unusual rulers of Germany. He avoided war, built fairy-tale castles, often went among his people incognito, and rewarded anyone who was "unknowingly" kind to him. He never married and so left no heirs.

To Germans, he was "our darling King." To others, he was "Mad" King Ludwig, obsessed with building a castle that would be a man-made extension of a mountain. "Where nature ends," he supposedly said, "I begin."

Neuschwanstein was Ludwig's retreat from life, where everything was perfect and beautiful, and where his dreams and Richard Wagner's operas came to life. Here, he could live like his heroes in operas and old German sagas.

At the end of his eccentric reign, the king withdrew completely from public life and spoke to his ministers only through his hairdresser. In 1886, Ludwig's uncle had him declared insane.

Right in the middle of Disneyland sits the famous Sleeping Beauty Castle. If you visit, you can see that it was modeled partly after Schloss Neuschwanstein.

—*R.K.D.*

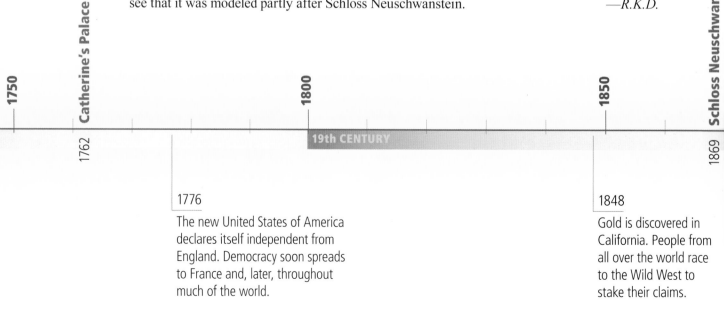

1750

Catherine's Palace

1762

1800

19th CENTURY

1850

Schloss Neuschwanstein

1869

1776

The new United States of America declares itself independent from England. Democracy soon spreads to France and, later, throughout much of the world.

1848

Gold is discovered in California. People from all over the world race to the Wild West to stake their claims.

Hearst Castle *California, United States, 1919*

Mothers know best: the builder and owner of Hearst Castle, William Randolph Hearst, had his mother to thank for inspiration. A dedicated teacher, she took her young son all over the world to explore her favorite castles—again and again.

Front page news: Hearst was the owner of one of America's richest business empires. It consisted of newspapers, magazines, and movie production companies. Now that's a media giant.

That's some present! Hearst was given his first newspaper, *The San Francisco Examiner,* when he was just twenty-three years old.

And you think homework is hard? Everything from nail to doorknob, from beam to brick, had to be shipped by boat to the pier at the base of the hills, then hauled up the winding, five-mile road on chain-driven trucks to the construction site. This American castle was under construction for more than twenty-five years!

Sleepover! Be ready to bunk in bell towers if the fifty other bedrooms are full. Don't forget your ear plugs! Bong, bong, bong ...

Jungle guest: Hollywood's Tarzan, Johnny Weissmuller, often visited Hearst Castle.

How would you like to own your own zoo? Hearst did. Kangaroos, giraffes, and zebras grazed freely on the lawns of his magnificent castle.   —*R.K.D.*

The Castle in the Air *A Viking Legend*

All of the castles in this book are real, except the last one, the Castle in the Air. Home to many myths, castles can be the dwelling places of gods and giants, fairies and fools, dwarfs and elves, monsters and maidens, knights and sorcerers, as well as kings and queens. The Castle in the Air is as imaginary as angels dancing on the head of a pin. You might even think of it as "pie in the sky."

Discovering this piece of "surreal estate" is like searching for the Fountain of Youth—a promise that can never be fulfilled. But when has that ever stopped anyone from trying? The two Eriks (one a Dane, the other a Norwegian, named I and II in the poem for convenience) boldly set out to do just that, even against the forces of prince-hungry dragons.

Odainsaker is the mythical "acre of the not-dead." When Erik of Norway climbed the Castle in the Air, he found a perfumed paradise resting on a lush, velvet carpet, and a gleaming table with the most delicious foods. But instead of staying forever in his soft bed there, he returned to tell his Viking kinsmen of all the wonders that he saw.   —*J.P.L.*

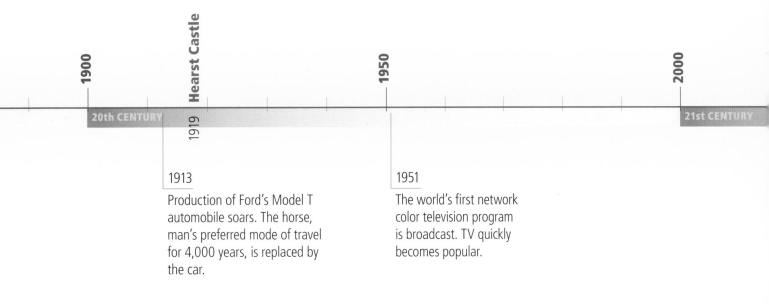

1900

Hearst Castle

1950

2000

20th CENTURY   21st CENTURY

1919

1913
Production of Ford's Model T automobile soars. The horse, man's preferred mode of travel for 4,000 years, is replaced by the car.

1951
The world's first network color television program is broadcast. TV quickly becomes popular.

Blackwood, Gary L. *Life in a Medieval Castle.* San Diego: Lucent Books, 2000.

Brooks, Laura. *Palaces: Masterpieces of Architecture.* New York: Todtri, 1999.

Castles. Mankato, MN: Creative Education, 1997.

Clements, Gillian. *The Truth About Castles.* Minneapolis: Carolrhoda Books, 1990.

Cormack, Patrick. *Castles of Britain.* New York: Crescent Books, 1982.

Dargie, Richard. *Knights and Castles.* Austin, TX: Raintree Steck-Vaughn, 1999.

Farré, Marie. *Long Ago in a Castle: What Was It Like Living Safe Behind Castle Walls?* Ossining, NY: Young Discovery Library, 1988.

Gibson, John. *Anatomy of the Castle.* New York: MetroBooks, 2001.

Gravett, Christopher. *Castle.* New York: Knopf, 1994.

Gravett, Christopher. *The History of Castles: Fortifications Around the World.* Guilford, CT: Pequot Press, The Lyons Press, 2001.

Howarth, Sarah. *The Middle Ages.* New York: Viking, 1993.

Johnson, Paul. *Castles of England, Scotland and Wales.* London: Weidenfeld and Nicolson, 1989.

Kastner, Victoria. *Hearst Castle: The Biography of a Country House.* New York: H. N. Abrams, 2000.

Langley, Andrew. *Medieval Life.* New York: Knopf, 1996.

Lee, Alan, and David Day. *Castles.* New York: Bantam Books, 1984.

Líbal, Dobroslav. *Castles of Britain and Europe.* Leicester, UK: Blitz Editions, 1999.

Macaulay, David. *Castle.* Boston: Houghton Mifflin, 1977.

Meltzer, Milton. *Ten Kings: And the Worlds They Ruled.* New York: Orchard Books, 2002.

Meltzer, Milton. *Ten Queens: Portraits of Women of Power.* New York: Dutton Children's Books, 1998.

Pipe, Jim. *Mystery History of a Medieval Castle.* Brookfield, CT: Copper Beech Books, 1996.

Sheehan, Sean. *Austria.* New York: Marshall Cavendish, 1993.

Wilkinson, Philip. *Castles.* New York: DK Publishing, 1997.

How Historians Date Castles

The dates you see on pages 40–47 are when the castles' *most important* construction occurred. You might ask, "Most important construction? What's that?" Castles, like houses, are often remodeled, torn down, and rebuilt. That makes it hard to assign one date for a castle's construction. If historians need to use a single date for a castle, they ask themselves when the most important construction occurred. (Maybe it was when a wall was built around the king's house or when a stone fortress replaced a wooden one.) Historians then use this most important construction date.

Think that was complicated? Try this: people often forget exactly when castles (or houses) were constructed. However, historians have ways to tell approximate dates. Sometimes they use a *c.* before a date, which means that construction occurred *circa* (Latin for "around") that date. Sometimes, when there is no record of a date, they just use the century.